All-American ★QUILTS★

Written by Biz Storms
Illustrated by June Bradford

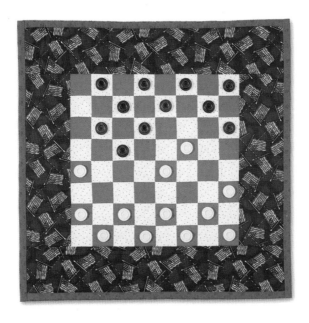

D1377560

KIDS CAN PRESS

To the men, women and children of the United States
— in celebration of their individual beliefs,
their right to expression and their personal freedom — B.S.

To my Mum and Dad, my husband, Stephen, and son, Keith,
for their continuing love, support and friendship — J.B.

Text © 2003 Biz Storms
Illustrations © 2003 June Bradford

KIDS CAN DO IT and the 📕 logo are trademarks of Kids Can Press Ltd.

Kids Can Press acknowledges the financial support of the Ontario Arts Council,
the Canada Council for the Arts and the Government of Canada,
through the BPIDP, for our publishing activity.

Published in Canada by
Kids Can Press Ltd.
29 Birch Avenue
Toronto, ON M4V 1E2

Published in the U.S. by
Kids Can Press Ltd.
2250 Military Road
Tonawanda, NY 14150

www.kidscanpress.com

Edited by Laurie Wark
Designed by Karen Powers
Photography by Frank Baldassarra
Printed in Hong Kong, China, by Wing King Tong Company Limited

The hardcover edition of this book is smyth sewn casebound.
The paperback edition of this book is limp sewn with a drawn-on cover.

US 03 0 9 8 7 6 5 4 3 2 1
US PA 03 0 9 8 7 6 5 4 3 2 1

National Library of Canada Cataloguing in Publication Data

Storms, Biz, 1955–
All-American quilts / written by Biz Storms ; illustrated by June Bradford.

(Kids can do it)
ISBN 1-55337-538-6 (bound).   ISBN 1-55337-539-4 (pbk.)

1. Quilting — Juvenile literature. I. Bradford, June II. Title. III. Series.
TT835.S746 2003   j746.46   C2002-905028-6

Kids Can Press is a *Corus*™ Entertainment company

Contents

LIBERTY

Introduction

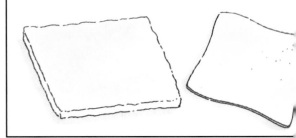

Celebrate your American spirit by stitching a patriotic quilt project. Start with a small quilt or pillow, or be inspired by the more challenging Log Cabin lap quilt. Share your patriotism, along with your red, white and blue fabrics, by quilting with a friend or starting a quilting group. Create with bright, vibrant fabrics, or work in soft pastel tones to stitch your special spirited design. Most important, be proud of your patriotic project — to commemorate your creativity, sew on a label (see page 19 for how to do this). Happy quilting.

MATERIALS

Gather these quilting supplies and store them in a box. You may find some of these items at home, or you can buy them at a quilt, craft or fabric shop.

Fabric

Buy new fabric or use leftover fabric that you have around home. Old shirts, pajamas and dresses make great quilting fabrics — 100% cotton works best. Wash new fabric before sewing to make sure the color doesn't run.

Quilt batting

Cotton batting is better than polyester because it is easy to cut and the edges don't fall apart. It comes in several sizes, so you can buy what you need. You may use cotton flannel instead, but your quilt will be flatter.

BASIC SEWING SUPPLIES

To work on the projects in this book, you will need these basic sewing supplies: scissors, needles, threads, pins, safety pins, an iron, a ruler, a pencil and masking tape.

Threads

Use 100% cotton for your threads and embroidery floss. When piecing your quilt together, use sewing thread, and pick a color that blends with your fabric. If you have several fabric colors, try beige or gray thread. If a project calls for embroidery floss, you can match it to your fabric or choose a contrasting color that really jumps out. Always separate the floss threads and use only two strands at a time. If you use more, the floss may knot or be too bulky. When quilting, use the thicker, waxed quilting thread or embroidery floss, and choose a color that you think looks best. White or ivory usually works well.

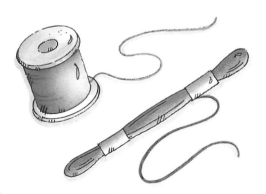

Needles

Use sewing needles, called sharps, for regular and quilting thread, and use embroidery needles for embroidery floss. A large eye for easy threading and a sharp point for smooth sewing are important. You can wear a thimble to help push the needle through the fabric. Metal and leather thimbles are available in different sizes. An adhesive bandage will work, as well.

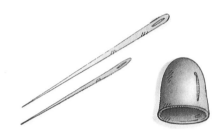

Pins

Straight pins with plastic or colored heads are easy to hold and see. Most projects call for safety pins. They should have a sharp point and be clear of rust.

Scissors

Use sharp scissors to cut fabric and thread. Small scissors are good for cutting thread and fit in your sewing box.

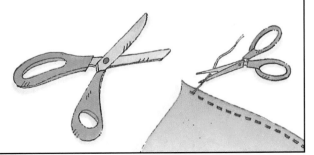

Pencils and a ruler

To mark cutting and sewing lines, you will need a lead pencil for light-colored fabrics and a white or silver pencil for dark fabrics. Sewing chalk or soapstone markers can also be used. You'll need a quilter's see-through ruler with ¼ in. (0.5 cm) increments to mark cutting lines and seam allowances.

Measuring

Measurements are given in both imperial and metric, which differ slightly. Choose one measurement system and use it for the entire project.

Iron and finger pressing

Always have an adult's help when using an iron. Use a regular iron on the cotton setting and press without steam. Your fingers can also do a good job of pressing and save you trips to the ironing board. Carefully press the seams between your thumb and index finger.

FUSIBLE WEB

Fusible web is a paper-backed adhesive that works with the heat of an iron to attach two pieces of fabric together. It is used mostly for appliqué projects. Pellon Wonder-Under, Steam-A-Seam or other brands are available. Check the label to make sure you can stitch through it. Before following the instructions below, read the manufacturer's directions because some brands use slightly different methods.

1. Trace or draw your appliqué shape onto the smooth, paper side of the fusible web.

2. Cut around the shape about ¼ in. (0.5 cm) outside the pencil line and remove unmarked paper backing.

3. Place your shape, rough or glue side down, on the wrong side of the fabric.

4. Fuse the web to the fabric with an iron.

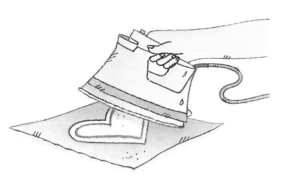

5. Cut out the shape along the pencil line.

6. Carefully peel off the paper backing.

7. Place your appliqué shape, glue side down, on the right side of the background fabric and fuse with an iron.

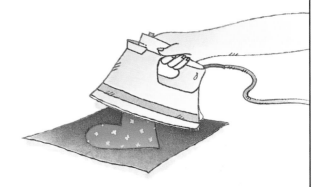

8. Blanket stitch (page 11) around the shape to secure the appliqué.

Quilting basics and stitches

Refer to these pages whenever you need sewing information. For assembling, or piecing, quilt blocks or tops (page 34), you may use a sewing machine instead of hand stitching. Read the Tips on page 22 for how to keep your quilt neat and clean.

Fabric sides

Printed fabric has two sides — the right side, with the pattern, and the wrong side, where the pattern is missing or faded. Solid and woven fabrics are not printed, so either side can show.

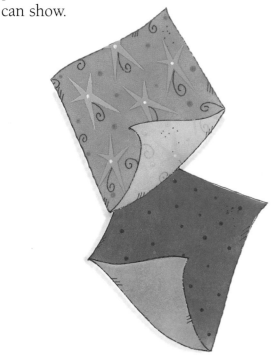

Seam allowance

A seam allowance is the distance between the edge of the fabric and the stitching line. Quilters usually use a 1/4 in. (0.5 cm) seam allowance. Draw the stitching line lightly with pencil on the wrong side of the fabric. You won't see the line on the finished project.

Threading and holding a needle

Cut about 18 in. (45 cm) of thread. Thread one end through the eye of the needle, leaving one end longer than the other. Hold the needle between your thumb and index finger. Use your middle finger to push the needle through the fabric.

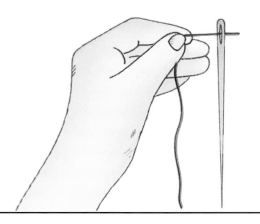

Loop knot

Begin and end seams with this knot.

1. Make a small stitch, leaving a
_ in. (2.5 cm) tail.

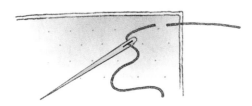

2. Backstitch (page 10) over the first
stitch but leave a tiny loop sticking up.

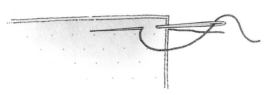

3. Slip the needle through the loop
from the top and pull the loop closed.

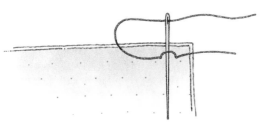

4. Make another backstitch and loop.
Slip the needle up from the bottom and
pull the loop closed. Trim the thread,
leaving a ¼ in. (0.5 cm) tail.

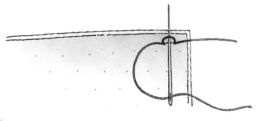

Running stitch

Use a small running stitch for seams and
a medium running stitch for quilting.

1. Start at a corner and push the needle
down through both layers of fabric.

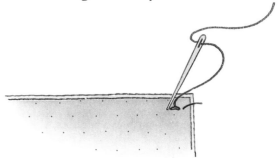

2. Bring the needle up through both layers
a short distance away and pull the thread
through. Repeat, making even stitches.

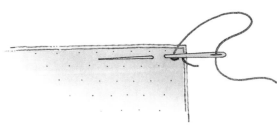

Changing thread

When you are running out of thread,
make a loop knot and leave a
¼ in. (0.5 cm) tail. With a new piece of
thread in the needle, make a loop knot
close to the last one and continue
sewing.

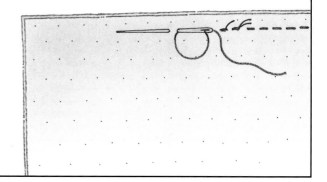

Backstitch

1. Make a small running stitch (page 9).

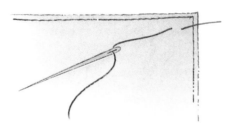

2. Make another stitch in the same spot, with the needle going in and out the same holes.

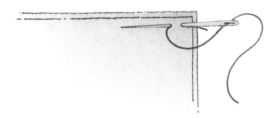

Blind stitch

This stitch is useful for sewing on a binding, a sleeve, a label or for closing a seam on a pillow.

1. Pin the label, sleeve or folded edge of fabric in place.

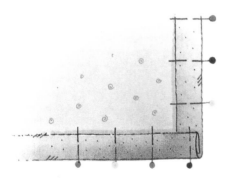

2. Make a loop knot (page 9) to the right-hand side (at the left-hand side if you're left-handed) of the opening or at a corner.

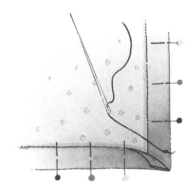

3. Start your stitch beside the loop knot and bring the needle up through the fabric fold a short distance away. Backstitch twice for a strong stitch.

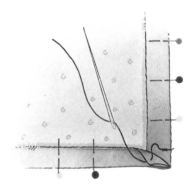

4. Continue with small, even stitches close to the folded edge. Finish with two backstitches and a loop knot.

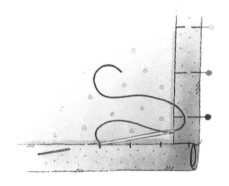

Blanket stitch

1. Using two strands of knotted embroidery floss, bring the needle up from the back of the fabric just outside the edge of the appliqué. Pull the floss through to the knot.

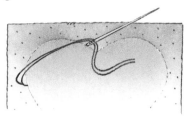

2. Hold the floss to the side of the appliqué with your thumb.

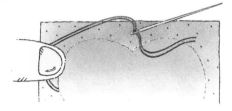

3. Insert the needle through the appliqué, about ¼ in. (0.5 cm) away. Bring the needle back out at the edge of the appliqué. Pull the needle above the floss held by your thumb.

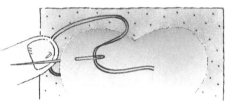

4. Release the floss and pull gently on the needle until the stitch lies flat.

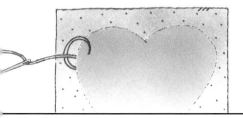

5. Repeat steps 2 to 4 as you stitch around the appliqué. Finish by pulling the floss to the back and making a loop knot (page 9).

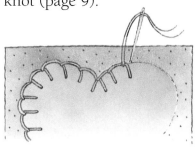

Sewing a seam

These are the basic steps for sewing a seam. The instructions for each project will tell you which stitch to use and when.

1. Pin two pieces of fabric right sides together.

2. Make a loop knot (page 9) at the right-hand side (at the left-hand side if you're left-handed).

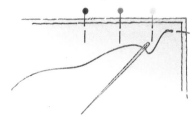

3. Using a small running stitch (page 9), sew to the other side.

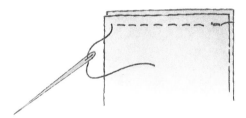

4. Make a loop knot. Cut the thread and remove the pins.

American eagle banner

The design for this 26 in. x 22 in. (66 cm x 56 cm) wall hanging was inspired by antique and Civil War quilts. It will look great hanging in your room or on your door.

YOU WILL NEED

- a 26 in. x 22 in. (66 cm x 56 cm) piece of background fabric
- a 31 in. x 27 in. (80 cm x 70 cm) piece of backing fabric
- a 28 in. x 24 in. (74 cm x 64 cm) piece of cotton batting
- fabric scraps for eagles, letters and sleeve
- fusible web
- embroidery floss
- 28 in. (71 cm) wood dowel or thin curtain rod
- basic sewing supplies (page 5)

1 Follow the instructions on page 6 to fuse and stitch the eagle, star and letters from pages 15, 39 and 40 to the background fabric.

2 Follow the instructions on pages 36 to 38 for layering, quilting and binding your quilt.

3 To form a sleeve for hanging the quilt, pin under ½ in. (1 cm) along each of the long sides of a 22 in. x 2 ½ in. (56 cm x 6 cm) scrap. Press with an iron and remove the pins.

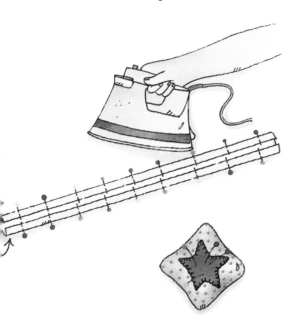

4 Blind stitch (page 10) the sleeve to the back of the banner below the top edge, right side out.

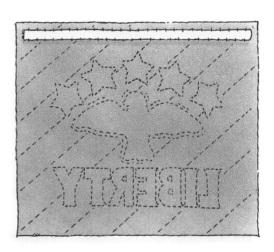

5 Slide a rod or dowel through the sleeve and hang your banner from pushpins or small nails.

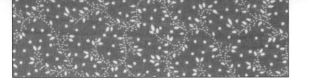

Liberty garden pillow

Turn a simple throw pillow into a patriotic statement. You may even want to add a yellow ribbon.

1 Follow the instructions on page 6 to fuse and stitch the appliqués to the background fabric. The star and leaf patterns are on page 15. Draw the stem shape freehand onto the fusible web.

2 Place the backing fabric wrong side up. Lightly pencil a ½ in. (1.5 cm) seam allowance on all four sides. Mark 10 in. (25 cm) opening on one side.

4 Turn the squares right side out and push the pillow form inside the pillow cover. Pin the opening shut and blind stitch (page 10) it closed. Remove the pins.

3 Pin the pillow top and the backing fabric right sides together. Using small running stitch (page 9), sew along all four pencil lines, leaving the 10 in. (25 cm) space open. Backstitch (page 10) several times at each side of the opening. Remove the pins.

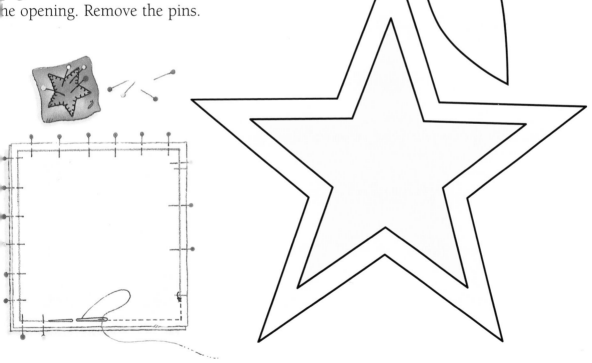

Patriotic pet quilt

Share your heartfelt patriotism with a family pet or a treasured stuffed animal. This 20½ in. (56 cm) square design is a great learn-to-quilt project for the beginning quilter.

- nine 4½ in. (12 cm) squares of background fabric
- two 4½ in. x 12½ in. (12 cm x 34 cm) strips of border fabric
- two 4½ in. x 20½ in. (12 cm x 56 cm) strips of border fabric
- fabric scraps
- a 26 in. (70 cm) square of backing fabric
- a 24 in. (64 cm) square of cotton batting
- fusible web
- embroidery floss
- basic sewing supplies (page 5)

1 Follow the instructions on page 6 to fuse and stitch the heart shape from page 17 onto the 4½ in. (12 cm) squares.

2 Follow the instructions on pages 34 to 38 for piecing the top, with borders, through to binding the quilt.

- Fuse and blanket stitch some heart blocks to a sweatshirt.

- Use light-colored fabric for an appliqué and write a special message on it with permanent ink.

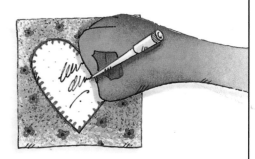

- If this quilt is for a cat, toss some catnip between the layers of fabric and batting before pinning the layers.

Stars and Stripes checkerboard

This 25½ in. (65 cm) square gameboard is perfect for traveling. Use large buttons, bottle caps or even cookies as game pieces.

YOU WILL NEED

- thirty-two 2½ in. (6 cm) squares of light-colored fabric
- thirty-two 2½ in. (6 cm) squares of dark-colored fabric
- two 5 in. x 16½ in. (13 cm x 40.5 cm) strips of border fabric
- two 5 in. x 25½ in. (13 cm x 65 cm) strips of border fabric
- a 30 in. (80 cm) square of backing fabric
- a 28 in. (73 cm) square of cotton batting
- basic sewing supplies (page 5)

1 With the right sides up, position the light and dark squares in a checkerboard pattern.

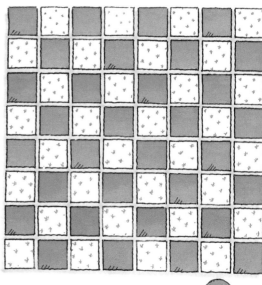

2 Follow the instructions on pages 34 to 38 for piecing the top, with borders, through to binding the quilt.

OTHER IDEAS

• You can use 2½ in. (6 cm) squares to create many designs. Try making diagonal rows of different colors or mixing up colors in a random pattern.

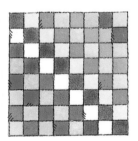

LABEL YOUR QUILT

Congratulations! You've finished your quilt project. Now it's time to make a label for it. Cut a 3½ in. (10 cm) square of light-colored fabric. Fold and iron ¼ in. (1 cm) from each side to the wrong side. Using permanent marker, print your name, the date, your city or town, and the title or name for your quilt. Pin the label to the back of the quilt and blind stitch (page 10) around it. Remove the pins.

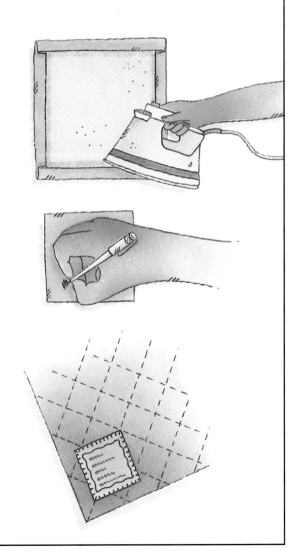

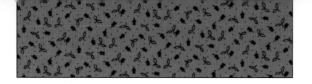

American flag

Combine your love of America with your passion for quilting, and create this family heirloom. Hang this 20 in. x 27½ in. (53 cm x 71 cm) flag on your front door or use it as a wall hanging.

- three 2 in. x 17 in. (5 cm x 43 cm) strips of white fabric
- four 2 in. x 17 in. (5 cm x 43 cm) strips of red fabric
- three 2 in. x 27½ in. (5 cm x 70 cm) strips of white fabric
- three 2 in. x 27½ in. (5 cm x 70 cm) strips of red fabric
- an 11 in. (29 cm) square of navy blue fabric
- light-colored fabric scraps
- a 26 in. x 34 in. (66 cm x 86 cm) piece of backing fabric
- a 24 in. x 32 in. (62 cm x 81 cm) piece of cotton batting
- fusible web
- embroidery floss
- basic sewing supplies (page 5)

1 Pin a 17 in. (43 cm) red strip and a 17 in. (43 cm) white strip, right sides together. Lightly pencil a ¼ in. (0.5 cm) seam allowance along the pinned edge.

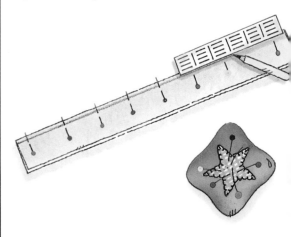

2 Sew along the pencil line with a small running stitch (page 9). Start and stop with a loop knot (page 9). Remove the pins.

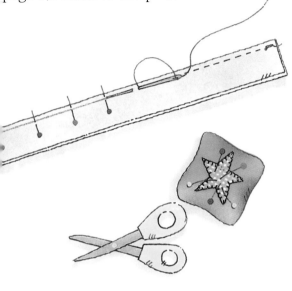

3 With the red fabric on top, flip open the strip and finger press the seam allowance behind the red.

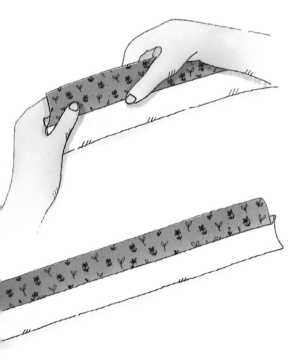

4 Repeat steps 1 to 3, alternating red and white strips, until all 17 in. (43 cm) strips are sewn together, with a red strip at the top and bottom. Press with an iron, keeping the seams straight.

5 Repeat steps 1 to 4 to sew the 27½ in. (70 cm) strips together, with a white strip at the top and a red strip at the bottom.

6 Fuse four white stars onto the navy square (page 6). Blanket stitch (page 11) around the stars. Place the three pieces together to look like the flag.

Instructions continue on the next page ☞

7 Pin the navy square to the 17 in. (43 cm) strips right sides together. Lightly pencil a ¼ in. (0.5 cm) seam allowance and stitch the pieces together with a small running stitch (page 9). Start and stop with a loop knot (page 9). Remove the pins, open and press with an iron.

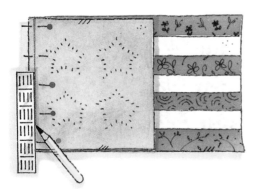

8 Pin the two halves right sides together. Mark the seam allowance, stitch and remove the pins. Flip the bottom half open and press the completed quilt top with an iron.

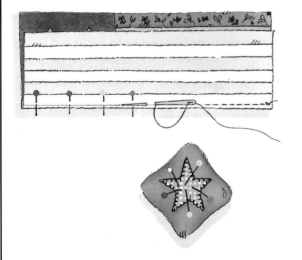

9 Follow the instructions on pages 34 to 38 for piecing, layering, quilting and binding the quilt.

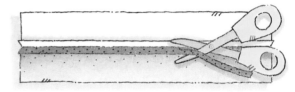

TIPS

- As you sew, trim loose threads and extra bits of fabric.
- If you have a seam allowance behind light-colored fabric and any dark fabric shows through, carefully cut the dark edges away.

- Iron the blocks before you sew them together, and the tops and backs before you layer them.
- Clean hands and a clean sewing space will protect your fabrics from getting dirty.

Friendship Star dresser quilt

This spirited quilt looks terrific in any combination of red, white and blue. The finished size is 20½ in. (51 cm) square.

YOU WILL NEED

- thirty-two 2½ in. (6 cm) squares of background fabric
- four 2½ in. (6 cm) squares of star fabric
- sixteen 2 in. (5 cm) squares of star fabric
- two 4½ in. x 12½ in. (12 cm x 31 cm) strips of border fabric
- two 4½ in. x 20½ in. (12 cm x 51 cm) strips of border fabric
- a 26 in. (66 cm) square of backing fabric
- a 24 in. (60 cm) square of cotton batting
- basic sewing supplies (page 5)

1 To make a star point, pin a 2 in. (5 cm) square of star fabric to a corner of a background square right sides together. Pencil a line from corner to corner on the small star square, as shown.

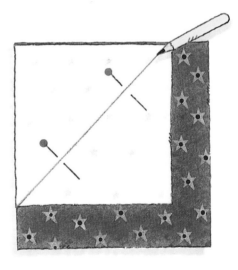

Instructions continue on the next page ☞

2 Sew along the pencil line with a small running stitch (page 9). Start and stop with a loop knot (page 9). Remove the pins, flip open the inside triangle toward the outer corner and finger press.

3 Cut out the middle triangle, leaving a ¼ in. (0.5 cm) seam allowance.

4 Repeat steps 1 to 3 to sew three more star points.

5 Place four star-point squares, four background squares and one star fabric square together as shown to complete a Friendship Star block.

6 Repeat steps 1 to 5 to make three more Friendship Star blocks.

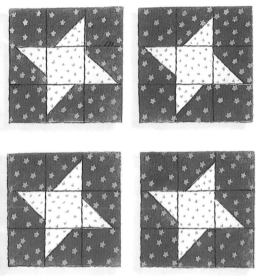

7 Follow the instructions on pages 34 to 38 for piecing the top, with borders, through to binding the quilt.

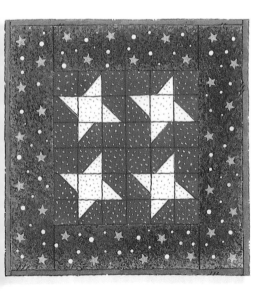

☆ ☆ ☆ ☆ ☆ ☆ ☆ ☆ ☆ ☆

OTHER IDEAS

- Add extra star blocks to make a table runner.

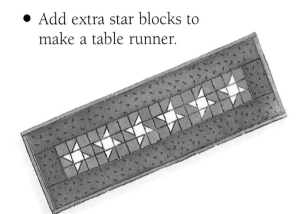

- Make a placemat by sewing together two blocks and adding borders (page 35).

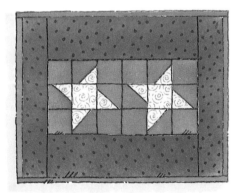

- Turn a single block into a small throw pillow.

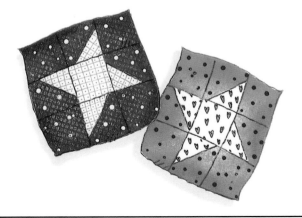

Log Cabin
lap quilt

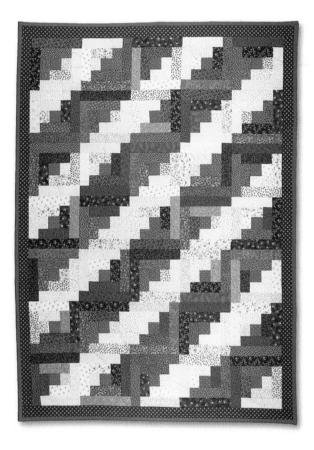

The traditional Log Cabin is one of the most popular quilt patterns in America's history. Your lap quilt will measure 41 in. x 56 in. (111 cm x 151 cm).

1 Pin a 2 in. (5 cm) light strip along one edge of a red square right sides together. Lightly pencil a ¼ in. (0.5 cm) seam allowance.

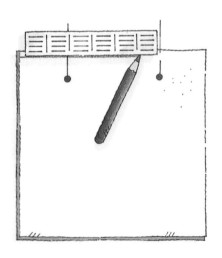

2 Sew along the pencil line with a small running stitch (page 9). Start and stop with a loop knot (page 9). Remove the pins, flip open the top strip and finger press. Lay the block right side up, with the light strip at the top.

3 Pin a 3½ in. (9 cm) light strip along the right side of the block right sides together. Pencil the seam allowance, stitch, remove the pins and finger press. Lay the block right side up, with the longest strip at the top.

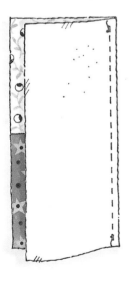

4 Pin a 3½ in. (9 cm) dark strip along the right side of the block right sides together. Pencil the seam allowance, stitch, remove the pins and finger press. Lay the block right side up, with the longest strip at the top.

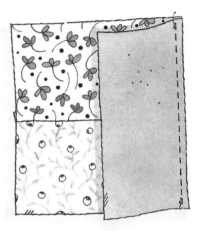

5 Repeat, adding a 5 in. (13 cm) dark strip. Press the block with an iron.

Instructions continue on the next page ☞

6 The block should be 5 in. (13 cm) square. If it's smaller, your seam allowance is too big. If it's larger, your seam allowance is too small. Adjust to sew a ¼ in. (0.5 cm) seam allowance, so the remaining strips will fit.

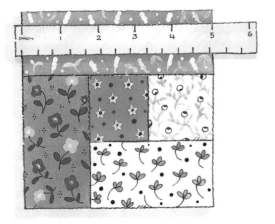

7 Lay the block right side up with the longest strip at the top. Repeat steps 1 to 5, using a 5 in. (13 cm) light strip, a 6½ in. (17 cm) light strip, a 6½ in. (17 cm) dark strip and an 8 in. (21 cm) dark strip. Press with an iron.

8 Your block should be 8 in. (21 cm) square.

9 Make thirty-four more blocks.

10 Follow the instructions on pages 34 to 38 for piecing the top, with borders, through to binding the quilt.

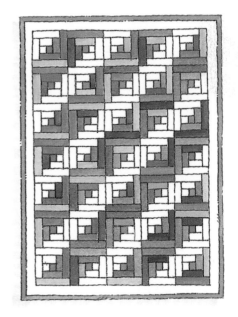

LOG CABIN PATTERNS

The light and dark sides of the Log Cabin block can be moved around to create many designs. These are four popular patterns. The design shown in the photograph on page 26 is called Fields and Furrows.

Streak of Lightning

Flying Geese

Roman Blind

Japanese Lantern

All-American sampler

This Americana sampler combines patriotic elements from other projects in this book. The finished size is 38 in. x 50 in. (98 cm x 128 cm).

1 Follow the instructions on page 6 to fuse and stitch the eagle, star and letters from pages 39 to 40 to the background fabric. Place the shapes as shown.

2 To make the four Friendship Star cornerstones, follow steps 1 to 6 on pages 23 to 25.

3 To make the striped borders, place the fabric strips together as shown.

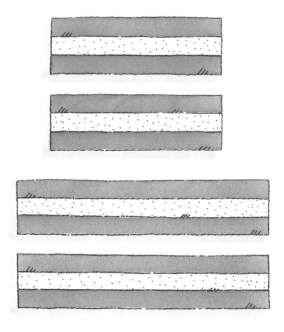

4 Follow steps 1 to 4 on pages 20 to 21. Complete all four striped borders.

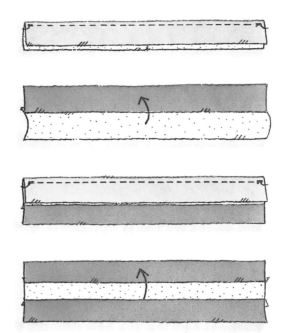

5 Place all the pieces together as shown.

6 Pin a 38 in. (98 cm) border to a long side of the center panel right sides together. Lightly pencil a ¼ in. (0.5 cm) seam allowance. Sew along the line with a small running stitch (page 9). Start and stop with a loop knot (page 9). Remove the pins. Flip open the border and press with an iron.

7 Repeat with the remaining 38 in. (98 cm) border on the opposite side. Place the pieces back together.

8 Pin a Friendship Star block to each end of a 26 in. (68 cm) border right sides together. Pencil the seam allowance, stitch and remove the pins. Flip open the blocks and press with an iron.

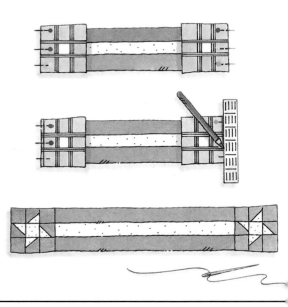

9 Repeat with the other 26 in. (68 cm) border and Friendship Star blocks. Place the pieces together.

10 Pin the top border to the center panel right sides together. Pencil the seam allowance, stitch and remove the pins. Flip open the border and press with an iron.

11 Repeat with the last border on the bottom of the center panel.

12 Follow the instructions on pages 34 to 38 for piecing, layering, quilting and binding the quilt.

Finishing your quilt

Follow the steps on the next five pages to finish your quilt.

PIECING

Follow these steps to assemble, or piece, a quilt top made from any number of blocks. If your quilt top is made with appliqués on a background, skip ahead to Adding Borders.

1 Lay blocks on a flat surface. Move them around until you like the way they look. Separate them into rows.

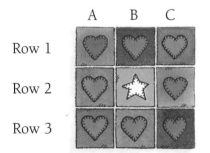

2 In row 1, pin blocks A and B, right sides together, where they meet. Pencil a 1/4 in. (0.5 cm) seam allowance. Sew along the pencil line with a small running stitch (page 9). Start and stop with a loop knot (page 9). Remove the pins.

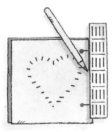

3 Press the seam open with an iron and put the stitched blocks back where they came from. Make sure the design is still correct. Sew block C to B, as shown.

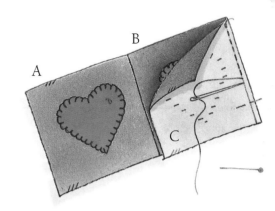

4 Repeat steps 1 to 3 to sew the remaining rows together.

5 Pin rows 1 and 2, right sides together, with the seams lining up. Pencil a 1/4 in. (0.5 cm) seam allowance. Sew along the pencil lines with a small running stitch (page 9), and backstitch (page 10) when you stitch across a seam line. Start and stop with a loop knot (page 9). Remove the pins.

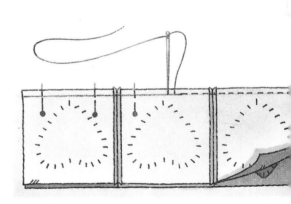

6 Press the seam open with an iron and put the stitched rows back where they came from.

1

2

7 Repeat steps 5 and 6 to finish the quilt top. Press with an iron.

ADDING BORDERS

Adding a border to your quilt top is optional. These instructions work for any size of quilt.

1 Position the border strips and the quilt top together the way you want the quilt to look.

2 Pin a side border to a side edge of the quilt top right sides together. Pencil a ¼ in. (0.5 cm) seam allowance.

3 Stitch along the pencil line with a small running stitch (page 9). Start and stop with a loop knot (page 9). Remove the pins, flip open the border and press with an iron. Repeat steps 2 and 3 with the border on the opposite side.

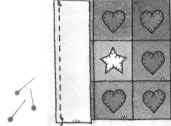

4 Repeat steps 2 and 3 with the top and bottom borders.

LAYERING

Every quilt needs to be layered. Use thick batting for a puffy quilt. Use a single layer of flannel or cotton batting for a thin quilt.

1 Iron the quilt backing then place it, right side down, on a flat surface. Tape down the corners and sides with masking tape.

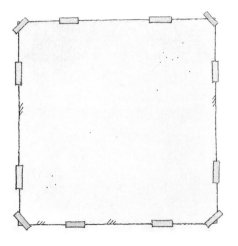

2 Place the batting in the middle of the backing, smoothing out the lumps and creases. Leave an even margin on all sides.

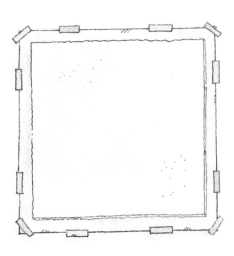

3 Iron the quilt top and lay it, right side up, on the batting, leaving an even margin on all sides.

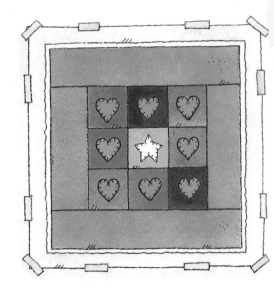

4 Use safety pins to pin the quilt layers together. Space the pins about 4 in. (10 cm) apart. Remove the tape.

QUILTING

Quilting stitches hold the three quilt layers together. Choose one of the designs shown here, purchase a quilting template or create your own design.

Use a light pencil line, sewing chalk or a soapstone pencil to mark the design lines. With either quilting thread or embroidery floss, use a medium running stitch (page 9) along the lines. Start and stop with a loop knot (page 9) close to the edge, so the knots will be hidden under the binding. If you need to change thread partway through a line or when quilting around appliqué, put the knots on the back of the quilt. Remove the safety pins as you sew.

- An appliqué template used for the quilt top can also be used as a quilting pattern.

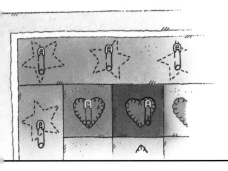

- A simple grid works well for quilts made with blocks. Pencil an X from corner to corner on each block. These X's will form a large grid pattern. Start stitching on one side of the quilt top and work your way across to the other side.

- For appliqué quilts, quilt around the appliqué, ⅛ to ¼ in. (0.25 to 0.5 cm) away from the edge. Add a grid of diagonal lines in the background.

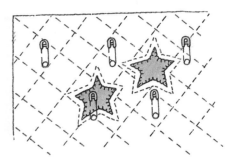

- Create a wavy line following the lines of the block or quilt top.

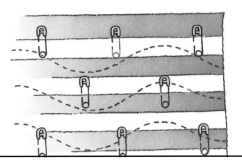

BINDING

1 Trim the batting to the edges of the quilt top. Be careful not to cut the backing fabric.

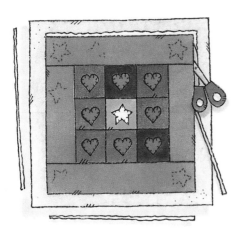

2 On each side of the quilt, cut the backing fabric to a width of ¾ in. (2 cm) for a narrow binding up to 2 in. (5 cm) for a wide binding. On opposite sides of the quilt, fold the edge in half. Press with an iron. Fold again over the top of the quilt to cover the raw edge. Pin in place.

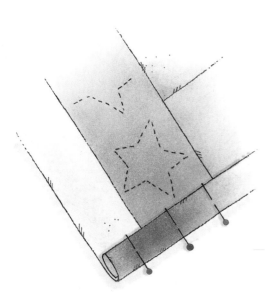

3 Fold, press and pin the other sides. Be sure the corners lie flat and have a clean edge.

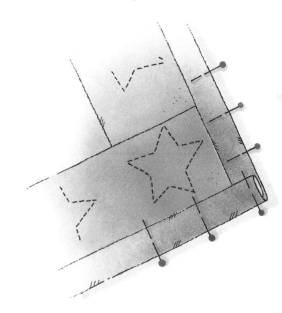

4 Blind stitch (page 10) the folded edges of the binding to the quilt top. Start and stop with a loop knot (page 9). Remove the pins.

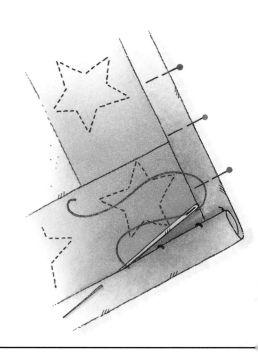

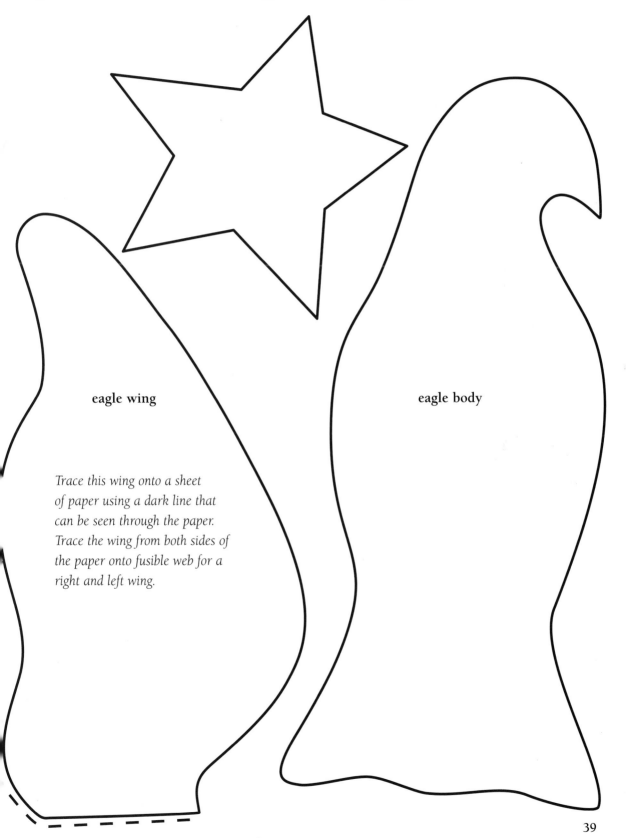

eagle wing

eagle body

Trace this wing onto a sheet of paper using a dark line that can be seen through the paper. Trace the wing from both sides of the paper onto fusible web for a right and left wing.

Note: *These letters will not appe backwards once you have fused them to the background fabric.*